Do You Even

Think

Before You Speak?

UNZIPPED

Also by Jocelyn G. Donahoo

The Cookie Cutter House

Do YOU even THINK Before YOU Speak?

UNZIPPED

Jocelyn G. Donahoo

Published by jgd & ice cream
Printed by Createspace, an Amazon.com Company

Also available on the Kindle.

Cover picture: Jocelyn G. Donahoo & Dante R. Donahoo

Author picture: Cynthia LuvbabyLuv

ISBN-13: 978-1544897752
ISBN-10: 1544897758

⌘

For *Nia,*

My outspoken, wise and articulate, nine-year-old granddaughter, who advised me to not worry about what other people think.

Acknowledgements

Thanks to God for allowing one door to close, but another to open; my husband Carl, a.k.a. Honey, for staying on me to publish a book of poetry; my mother, Pauline Elizabeth Foster, who helps me from the other side, for instilling her spirit of "doing things her way," embracing being unconventional, and not being a follower. Some may refer to it as stubborn, but you've got to respect an independent spirit. Special recognition goes to Donna and Izabella Wilke for the typography and lips cover concept, my son Dante, who worked tirelessly on turning my numerous requests to a reality for my beautiful cover and troubleshooting the interior layout; Lauren Scharhag, for rescuing me and my sanity and formatting my table of contents, although I chose to use a different style; Cynthia LuvbabyLuv, who captured a good angle of me reciting poetry that I used for my author photo; Alissa Butler and Prudence Washington for making sure I crossed every "t" and dotted every "i." Last but not least, too many to name, my family, friends, and admirers of my poetry, who compliment and encourage me. Thanks for your overwhelming support. And because I love you, here goes an official out of birth order shout out to my Hoo Crew : my international son Armand, Dante, Tia, Josiah, Nia, Nyla, Dario, Kim, Auburn, Jordan, Alexander, Yeilin, Kevin, Carl, Kayra, Justus, Joshua, Caleb, Kywana, and Ronnell. A special wink to Dr. Jason White, thanks for having my back on more than one occasion.

There is one whose rash words
are like sword thrusts,
but the tongue of the wise brings healing.
Proverbs 12:18 ESV

Table Of Contents

15
UNSHACKLED TONGUE

17
Do You Even Think Before You Speak

19
Reality Check

21
I See Color

24
They're Intimidated, Alienated, Frustrated?

26
It Goes Against My Christian Beliefs

27
Tight Schedule

29
QUIRKY WIT

31
This Goatee Is Too Much For Me

33
Snore Like A Tugboat

34
Girl, He Even Sucked My Toes

37
THE MS JOURNEY

39
The Blue One

42
I've Got This

44
With God's Grace And Mercy,
I Take Chances

46
That's The Way I'll Roll

35
The Beauty Of The Human Body's Work
And Command

50
God's Got My Back No Matter How High My Troubles
Are Stacked

53
I COULD EASILY LOSE MY MIND

55
A Crime Divine

57
Like Mayhem

58
The Kindle

60
Without Guilt Or Penalty

62
Stockpile, Stash Or Store

65
WHAT CAN I SAY, WE'RE FAMILY

67
Aren't You Al's Daughter?

69
Doing Things Her Way

71
The Stride Of Honey

73
We Called Him Mr. Foster

75
GUMBO

77
Not Your Average Color Guard

79
It's Been A Long Time Coming

81
Prince, Into The Cosmos

83
Female Folk Favor Fellowship

85
A Common End

Unshackled

tongue

⌘

Do You Even Think Before You Speak?

"Do you even think before you speak?"
My husband accused versus asked me.
 "No," I said scowling, my hands hugging my hips.
"Well, you need to start," he stressed,
shaking his head, looking in disbelief.

Yes, I've been faulted for having no filter,
The truth of the matter is
Some people don't like the truth,
Some people can't speak the truth,
While others won't even ponder the truth.

I've been told I wear my emotions on my sleeves.
Please.
Don't hate.
Can't help it's hard to deny or disguise
What I believe.

Have I learned from hurting people's feelings?
Not until mine were trampled over,
Requiring a supernatural healing.
A faux pas, a misstep, or blunder,
Is now replaced with consideration and love,

Restraining impulsive views provoked by an irresponsible tongue.

Reality Check

Every black man I know has been profiled.
You know, DWB or WWB.
Oh, you want me to clarify?
Driving or walking while black.
Hell, just *being* black!

Yeah, it was wrong for those brothers
to burn, loot, and destroy
their own neighborhoods.
But there comes a boiling point.
What would you do if
for centuries *your* people
have been hung, raped, oppressed?
Let's be real,
discriminated and exploited!

Travon Martin rightly hiked home from the store,
and was wrongly killed by a cop wannabe.
Michael Brown flexed
and instead of being arrested,
ended up in a casket.
Eric Garner sold cigarettes—
a misdemeanor,
but was choked down
screaming "I can't breath!"

He paid the ultimate price,
indicative of our lengthy
Emmitt Till like unfair history.

What takes the cake
is the statement that the officer made.
Freddie Gray simply made eye contact
and ran.
Sadly, he ended up slammed,
complaining of pain,
a severed spinal cord,
and eventually,
a reservation
in the morgue.

Black lives matter!
Martin worked for peace.
But sometimes, like Malcolm,
it takes "by any means necessary."
So don't talk to me
about thugs and beasts.
It's easy to judge
when some people,
my people,
aren't seen as human beings.

I See Color

"I don't see color," she said,
sincerely.
I noticed a few side eyes, eye rolls, and smirks.
Evidence that they perceived it was a quirk.
My thought was
excuse me
but I beg to disagree.
"Cause if a couple of brothas with sagging pants and
oversized hoodies
crossed your path,
and you found yourself outnumbered,
and you clutched your purse,
and you crossed the street,
would you still say or believe that?

Years ago in a 200—seat college lecture hall,
a friend brought something to my attention.
"Jojo," she whispered,
"we're the only two black people in here."
Having grown up in inner city Detroit
watching our neighborhood go from diversified to
white flight
taking exodus, segregating the races to the suburbs.
Scrutinizing the students up and down the aisles,
I had to do a double take.

Eyebrows furrowed, I replied,
"Oh . . . you're right," amazed she felt self-conscious,
as if she didn't belong,
as if she'd fallen for that Jim Crow rhetoric.

I see color.
Does it affect how I treat or come at you?
No.
I have a right to be wherever I am,
unless you make me feel uncomfortable,
or less than.
It makes no difference to me.
I'm going to speak to whoever is near
having no fear.

I see color.
How can you not?
God made all these beautiful things that we glory in:
the emerald colored water rolling over
snowy white sand,
that relaxes your shoulders and
soothes your digestion;
golden yellow sunflowers with the dark brown centers
that brighten your day;
candy apple red cars, and
that's only the beginning.

When it comes to skin tone,
that's where God designed
a plethora of color scheme pallets.
Black—African origin skin
covers a great deal of the color wheel:
Ivory—almost white, albino,
Olive, high yellow—butter cream,
Butterscotch, golden tan,
Café au lait, cinnamon,
bronze, pecan tan,
cocoa, coffee,
ebony, mahogany,
so many shades to see
celebrating our diversity.

While some took offense,
I understood her seemingly insincere pretense.
She meant no harm.
She wanted us to know that
she's inclusive,
and
doesn't judge people
based on the cover of their book,
by the color
of their skin.
It makes no sense.

They're Intimidated, Alienated, Frustrated?

"They're intimidated, alienated, frustrated."
That's what Governor Kaisch (kay-shh) stated
about the *crazies* who went on a rampage
and *terminated* innocent men, women, and our youth.

There was a time when we respected our elders.
School and college, *was* a place to learn.
A movie theater, *was* a place for entertainment.
Church, *was* a place of refuge, a safe haven.
But not any more.

Now there's a lethal threat.
It's become commonplace
to shoot at and even *murder*
our law enforcers, our sheriffs,
our *peace* officers,
the ones who serve to defend us.

Is history repeating itself?
Are we back to the wild, wild, west,
the Al Capone prohibition days
where everybody is open prey,
even those who vowed

to put their lives on the line?

I sat in the Raider Arena
amongst a group of grievers
offering to pay our respect
to an officer, who for many like me,
was a complete stranger.

And yet, one by one,
we men, women, and children,
some from afar, some from nearby,
some in uniform, some not,
some related, some just standing in the gap,
stood or sat,
dabbing or wiping our teary eyes
mourning, least we forget.
Which left me shaking my head
pondering the question,
"They're intimidated, alienated, and frustrated?"
Hel-lo . . . "What . . . is going on?"

It Goes Against
My Christian Beliefs

What must it be like
to be inside of a body
whose mind is mismatched
and doesn't feel right?
To be teased and beaten,
because haters please.

It goes against
my Christian beliefs.
And yet,
who am I to judge?
Jesus said
we should love.

Tight Schedule

Everybody is *so* busy!
We make promises
to call, to do lunch,
it's hit or miss.

We call and play phone tag you're it
between phone lines
and wi-fi.

It's really sad.
We neglect
our homebound elders,
and family, *and* dear friends.

When *all* it takes is a brief tap,
push a button,
no longer the effort of dialing the phone
to drop a dime and spend some time.

Are we *so* busy
that we will be filling our jar of regrets
with I wish I would'da, could'da . . . should'da?

When *all* it took was
"Hey, how ya doin'?

⌘

QUIRKY WIT

⌘

This Goatee Is Too Much For Me

At first, I plucked
the unwanted black and white weeds.
Now, like my husband,
I pick up the edger
and glide over
the obstinate hedges.
I've always had a mustache,
but this goatee
is too much for me.

Thoughts of 1984
are crystal clear,
but a mere minute ago,
I don't know.
Can't remember a short-term thing.
It didn't hurt my feelings
when my menses
ceased.

Just didn't fathom
the furnace would ignite,
switch my mojo
from hot to cold,

and change my interest
of erotic play to plight.
Surely, couldn't foresee
my heart pounding out of my chest,
my energy running low
requiring a mid-day doze,
or that a cough or sneeze
can trigger a wiggle
with the need to be relieved.

So I pause for the cause—
consolation . . . menopause.

Snore Like A Tugboat Horn

He snores like a tugboat
sounding its horn
as it hauls
an oil barge ashore.

His cyclic respirations
with a 9-second-cessation
keeps her conscious
and on full observation.

He awakens tired,
irritable, and peeved
after snuggling bits
of tormented sleep.

His complaint of fatigue
is finally relieved
with a mask and a hose
covering his nose.

She rejoices
and yet, there's only one regret
Darth Vader
is sleeping next to her.

"*Girl*, He Even Sucked My Toes!"

"*Girl*, he even sucked my toes!"
I was sitting in the waiting room,
in the musical chairs line
of a "black" beauty shop.
One of the ones that has creative stylists
who over book,
and have you there for hours.
Who knows what you'll hear
when you're there.
There might be "Jer-ry, Jer-ry!"
on the TV,
or Rachel Ray making the recipe of the day.

I flipped through hairstylist magazines
deciding on which style I wanted to get.
Knowing good and well, it was an unrealistic wish.
I wouldn't look like the models.
They have different bone structure,
hair texture, and length.
Of course, that was years ago,
because now, all you need
is enough hair to be pinched, braided, or twisted.
Maybe not even that, since the use of glue
is a cinch.

My mind took a dive on the curiosity side,
wondering what else was on the menu.
If Honey sucked my, I mean,
"he" sucked "her" toes,
what other parts were included in her throes?
I ended up going to a Christian,
more professional salon,
with gospel songs and PG programming,
where time was respected and abided by.
But every now and then,
I slip up and hear
"*Girl*, he even sucked my toes!"

⌘

THE MS JOURNEY

⌘

The Blue One

I shuffled in the door,
slid over to the sofa,
and before I could even plop down,
the frayed strand finally snapped.
Sobbing, shoulders shaking, stomach quivering,
I grieved.

Well, I hope he's satisfied.
This should ensure he got what he wanted.
"You should go and get one.
It'll make your life much easier," he'd harped.
He just didn't understand what it meant.

I'm not so prideful I can't accept help.
But I'm a nurse, the one who *provides* assistance.
It would leave me at a disadvantage.
The next step would mean admitting I was less than.
Labeled disabled.

I held it in my hand,
examined the blue color,
and knew deep down inside,
it had been *six* months.

It was the mall incident that sealed my fate.

Loaded down with bags near JC Penney's,
fatigue engulfed me.
Tired, weak, and frustrated, I stumbled, again.
It was a chore to coordinate
my anything but military cadence,
each foot off pace.
"God, if you just let me make it to my car,
I *promise* you, I'll acquire one."

Clutching onto strangers' vehicles,
staggering like a drunk,
I all but crawled to my car.
Lesson learned.
The next day, I got my doctor's signature
on the mandatory form with a check on "g"—
Severe limitation in a person's walking ability
due to an arthritic, neurological,
or orthopedic disorder,
then headed straight to the DMV,
and obtained the "red" *Temporary* one.

Drained of regrets and self-doubt,
I inhaled a deep breath,
rocked to get my momentum,
pushed off the sofa, and stood up.
It was time to fix dinner.
Truth be told, life *is* so much easier.

Besides, it's not the end of the world.
Numerous people have a "blue" *permanent*
parking placard.

I've Got This

Funny how people look at *me*,
frowning and confused,
when they offer to help
and I tell them,
"I got this."

Their intentions to politely push open doors
causing missed clearance on my canes,
or offers to
lift up my walker over a curb,
while I'm still leaning my entire body weight
on the black rubber tires
that rotate
producing a hindrance to keep my balance.

You see
I really do appreciate
their intended assistance.
But I'd rather not fall.
I've got this.
People talk about me,
but I watch my husband take offence
when someone volunteers
to extend an arm or a hand,
open a door,

carry my bag, better yet, fetch a chair,
while he's standing right there.

Or my son Armand,
when he's backing my wheelchair
up a step on the sidewalk,
and someone proposes to assist with the lift.
Whether they get it consciously or subconsciously,
somehow it's not perceived as rude or crude,
when they *too* say,
"I've got this."

With God's Grace And Prayer, I Take Chances

Look at me.
I walk hunched over,
slow, stiff, one unsteady foot
ahead of the other,
with a walker.
Or not one, but *two* canes.
And many wonder
"how do you do it?"

I'm not an inspiration
to you.
I take chances.
The evidence
is in the scars, bumps,
and bruises on my body
trying to prove my individuality.

Some wonder how I've accepted
this fate and kept my sanity.
Not once have I asked the Lord,
"why me?"
Yes, sometimes I have challenging days,
"weak" days,

but I have to press . . . any way.
And the press . . . is prayer:
standing tall and erect at the altar . . . dignified prayer,
"Lord if you, I promise I'll" . . .
private deal making prayer,
"Lord you said" . . . fussing, angry prayer,
"Hallelujah! . . . thankful, exalting prayer,
"Please Lord" . . . begging and pleading—
even whining prayer,
they all get me through.
I have no shame.
God doesn't judge,
he just wants the truth.

Perhaps I could avoid
physical and emotional pain,
if only I heeded
what my body needed.
But, I'm not an inspiration
to you.
With God's grace and prayer,
I take chances.

That's The Way I'll Roll

I cannot deny my disappointment
about the possibility of *temporarily*
losing the latitude
to put my pedal to the metal,
to spin the steering wheel,
to go on whatever journey
whenever I please.

I must change my mindset.
Re—think.
Re—learn.
Execute in another form
that which I've been doing
since I was fif—teen.

Instead of using my dysfunctional feet,
I'll accelerate and brake
with hand controls,
and that's
the way
I'll roll.

The Beauty
Of The Human Body's
Work And Command

Standing on my feet preparing a meal
often requires a much needed—legs elevated,
core and posture resting break.
Seems like no big deal
for those whose body moves steadily like a wheel.
Some folks can't comprehend
the beauty
of the human body's work
and command.

Once a single trip to the commode
caused my legs to noodle down to the ground.
After several unsuccessful attempts to hoist myself up,
I was incapacitated.
And my mind laughed and screamed,
"I've fallen and I can't get up!"
But it's no joke, suffering this cup,
of trying to get up off the ground
when there's no one around.
Some folks don't appreciate
or understand
the beauty of the human body's

work and command.

Having to scoot across the floor,
try *three* times to stand,
and not have my body *obey*
what I say,
left me in a state of helplessness
to grasp my inability
to complete
a simple
physical task.
Listen folks, the beauty
of the human body's work
and command, is incomparable.

I'm definitely not as brave as I once thought,
romancing about taking chances.
Not when my Honey had to lift me up,
plop my legs across the bed,
and I have neither the capability
to lift my legs, point or flex my toes.
I didn't know what to expect
or what was next.

Some folks don't appreciate
or understand
the beauty

of the human body's work and command.
But the moral of this story
is one of faith.
You see,
I humbled myself.
A retch like me.
I prayed without ceasing.
All.
Night.
Long.

And when I woke up,
I could lift my legs,
and point and flex my toes.
Only God knows and can resolve our woes.
And I don't care if you think I'm preaching.
Folks, this is no joke,
appreciate and understand
the beauty
of the human body's work and command.
It's God's master plan.

God's Got My Back
No Matter How High
My Troubles Are Stacked

What makes me happy?
Knowing God's got my back
no matter how high my troubles are stacked.
The sun—makes me feel bright, alive, and fun.
The stars and moon—look up at night,
they make me swoon.
Ice cream is the food of my dreams.
Cleansing my countenance with bright colors of
cinematic life
that make me feel happy and avoid strife.
joHoney—despite that jaded look on his face,
he's the funniest thing around my place.
My grands: they sing, they dance,
they wrestle, are musical,
athletic, academic,
their abilities are systemic!
My children: are great fathers, friends—awesome
men.
Their partners: are mentors, mothers, confidants—
wise wives.
My friends: because they accept me just as I is.
The list could go on and never end.

Think and look around.

Avoid things that make you frown.

What's at stake? Learn from your mistakes.

The Word says, in I Thessalonians 5:16-18, "Rejoice always.

Pray without ceasing. In everything give thanks."

This command is not a prank.

Why bother? Because the adversary

sneaks and peeks into that crack of unbelief.

But I've got a remedy for the enemy.

Smile.

Even when you don't want to.

Smile.

You hurt, you feel defeated?

Smile.

In need of food, clothing, or shelter?

Call on the Helper.

Then smile.

No job, bills piling up?

Smile.

Got a job, with anything but ideal conditions?

Prepare for your new position.

Smile.

Mate won't cooperate?

Refuse to berate.

Smile.
Kids acting a fool?
School them with the parental rules.
And smile.

When you can't even utter God's Word,
The intercessor, the Holy Spirit is heard.
Smile.
Kirk Franklin said it best,
"You look so much better when you oh, oh, oh."
So smile.
God's your back no matter how high
your troubles are stacked.

Now go into your pocket,
draw out your smile,
paste it firmly on your face,
and believe it or not
it'll cooperate.
Smile.

I COULD EASILY LOSE MY MIND

⌘

A Crime Devine

It's a crime
for something to taste so fine.
You bring me pleasure
of which I can't measure.
I could easily loose my mind,
for you my absolute treasure.

I can't negate how I like to celebrate
holidays, birthdays, even funerals with you.
Combined and conjoined
with some chocolate cake,
if I didn't have you,
I wouldn't have a clue.

One week's consumption
causes my hips and thighs
to increase in size.
And that's my prize?
Fat's how you come equipped.
You could easily be my demise.

Happy or sad,
up or down,
tight or closed,

Ice cream,
you're the only one that knows.

Like Mayhem

Sitting in the bleachers,
he's fidgety, restless.
He stands up.
He sits down.
His wiggly legs
bump mine.
He steps and stumbles on my toes,
as he attempts to pass by down the row,
carefully toting nachos whose peppers
tickle my nostrils.

"Is it over yet?" is his hopeful request.
His parents smile
at their youngest child.
He asks to *play* tackle with his brother,
rather than witness this football game debacle.
Still he rocks and glides
to the sound of Eagle Pride.

Their youngest son,
he's unruly.
He's in motion all the time.
Is that why they sat below?
To get a breather
from their anything but obedient, hyper child?

The Kindle

I didn't want one.
It was cheating.

There's nothing like a bright, colorful book cover
that demands your attention as you pass a display,
or leaf through a collection
at a bookstore;
nothing like holding a book in your hand,
touching, feeling, and smelling the crisp pages.

I didn't buy it.
It was a gift.

So I had to accept it.
I dreaded the learning curve,
but I named it *Jo's World*,
and once I figured things out,
well, some things out,
this font issues sista'
celebrated the capability to
turn that hard to read
"8" or "10" font
into a legible "12" or "14."

Not to mention that helpful dictionary

at a simple touch of a finger.
I hate to admit it, but
I've caught myself
trying to do that very thing
with a book.
Yikes, look at me I'm a wannabe techy!

It is advantageous to have one.
Because "have app" can travel
with you via the cloud
on your laptop,
your tablet,
or your phone.
And I can even read in bed
when Honey insists,
"All lights out."

I accept I was once a skeptic.
But if the book font is cryptic,
or I want to read in the dark,
my Kindle is where I embark.

Without Guilt Or Penalty

It was my decision
to quickly write a revision.
It shouldn't take but a minute.
But if you're a writer,
well, you know
that minute . . . it overlapped,
and trampled my vow
of "dinner will be ready in an hour."

The problem is the voices.
Keeping up with the voices.
They can be distracting.
They crowd my head.
Pushing and shoving,
each and every character,
wanting some attention.

Unlike some writers, I don't outline.
The characters dictate the plotlines I create.
They force me into the zone.
Not the Twilight,
but the artistic, imaginative
up to three—four—five a. m. .

Keys can be heard pecking, computing:
wisecracking, face slapping,
roving over ruddy clay roads,
heart pounding, hairs rising on the back of the neck,
breathtaking views of a luminous red maple tree,

tears trailing down pudgy cheeks,
a kid smiling with jack-o-lantern-like teeth,
type verses and scenes.

So I guess, I just need to answer their bidding.
And let the words flow freely.
Without guilt or penalty.

Stockpile, Stash or Store

Papers loosely stacked
atop the bulging book case,
antiquated anecdotes
staying afloat in a sea
of "Great Mom," "Thanks," & love notes.

Earrings neatly arranged
in fishing bait trays,
knotted necklaces too troublesome to adorn,
beautiful bracelets and rings strewn
inside a dusty felt drawer.

Clothes basket brimming
with paystubs & receipts
from Cox Cable, Tricare, Chase —
invoices and important papers
so long outdated and obsolete.

The mention of giving the room attention
causes much dissension.
Never the right time
to address the heap
without an internal debate
of trash, donate, keep.

Some say it's sentimental.
Indecisive, yes.
She boards needless possessions.
And why,
is still the unanswered question.

Call it what you want:
stockpile, stash or store.
There's only one definition,
the justification complex
yet simple,
Hoarder.

⌘

WHAT CAN I SAY . . .
WE'RE FAMILY

⌘

Aren't You Al's Daughter?

Aren't you Al's daughter?
Ya look just like 'em.
Oh how those words used to BURN-ME-UP!
Why couldn't I look like Mama? My sister did.
Who wants to look like someone who left you
out to dry?
Never sent a birthday card, nor Christmas gift,
Not EVEN encouraging words . . .

Reminiscing . . .
Butterfly kisses . . .
The tickle of his mustache under my nose,
Dancing on the tips of his toes,
The rotten egg smell of Magic shaving powder,
His shaving brush in the medicine cabinet,
Umm, the hypnotizing smell of *Old Spice cologne*,
Him singing, "Shop at Paul's, Da-doo-da-doo-da-doo-
doo,"
Boy he could carry a tune,
"You're a good dancer like your dad," she'd always say,
His smooth, deep chocolate skin and thick mustache,
Two little girls kissing his army picture,
"We have the handsomest daddy
in the whole wide world."

"He talks about his kids in Detroit all the time,"
They'd say.
If that was the case,
Why did he leave us 3 kids for another 3 kids?
Couldn't find a job,
No money to take care of his family . . .
Hard times.
He was a broken man.
How was I supposed to **know**?

Reflections . . .
Dancing gives me great pleasure,
 "You sang that song melodiously," she said,
I love to challenge my voice to reach the right notes.
Deep, chocolate skin,
De' ja' vu,

Aren't you Al's daughter?

Doing Things Her Way

Tired of holding down a job by herself,
it was healthier to go it without him.
A single parent of three kids,
she worked the evening shift
to make the extra differential.

She sewed our shorts, skirts,
and dresses, made curtains and couch covers
comparable to Surefit. Even laid carpet.
Like a true country girl, she knew the soil,
grew cucumbers, tomatoes, and collards.

A jack-of-all-trades, she opted to troubleshoot
any household problem. Went beneath the sink
to fix a leak,
put her head under the hood
like an auto mechanic,
and changed the oil and spark plugs.

Taught us to ride a bike.
Drove us cross country biannually
from Detroit through the Jim Crow south
to Tallahassee. Always meeting our needs
and setting aside her own goals.

After a summer of her watching me

sweeping and mopping,
washing clothes, walls, and frying chicken,
driving her to doctor appointments, she waved
sitting in her wheelchair on the front porch,
as I said, "Goodbye" . . . never to see her breathing
again.

The Stride Of Honey

Honey colored light-skin, dark wavy hair,
The cool way he strides,
Shoulders back, arms swinging ever so slightly,
Emanates confidence.

The way his eyes permeate her skin,
As if she's his favorite, a delectable
Three scoop buttered pecan ice cream cone.

The way he moves his hand across his head
To press his black, wavy, silvery streaked hair
When he's thinking or tired.

The slow, sensual way he holds her close,
Pressing his body against hers
on the dance floor,
Sending an electric current flowing
Through her body.

The nervous laugh "aha-ha" he does,
When he's feeling
Jealous or insecure.

He is the honey colored,
Light skinned, wavy haired guy,

Who emanates confidence,
With his arms swinging, ever so slightly.

A cool stride,
My Honey.

We Called Him Mister Foster ♪

You could find him
sitting on the stump in front
of 629 West Virginia Street.
Between hocking up spit
like lobbing a soft ball,
he'd pull out a piece of Tops paper,
open his tobacco pouch,
take an ample pinch, align it,
lick a thick glob of slob,
and roll the uneven cigarette.
Saturated, it took a few attempts
to strike a match,
and keep the leaves lit.

Like a squirrel,
he had a hidden collection of possessions,
tucked in pockets and places,
that he rarely shared.
He often sat alone,
smoking and wearing a beater,
but welcomed company
when folks strolled by his home.
 "Al talks about y'all all the time,"
he often bragged,
about his oldest son,

my dad.

Funny, we rarely called him granddaddy.
But he was proud to call me his grandbaby
and say, "Come here and give me some shug-ga,"
with his raspy voice and rattling cough,
cigarette flopping between his full lips,
just inside his full mouth.
I'd drag my feet, sidestepping a brown bottle,
and give him a kiss on the cheek confessing,
"I love you, Mr. Foster."

♪ *1st Prize Winner of the 2016 James and Christian LaRoche Memorial Poetry Contest*

GUMBO

⌘

Not Your Average Color Guard ♪ ♪

She doesn't look like the average color guard.
She has some meat on dem bones:
a full chest, thick waist,
plump hips and thighs.
But it doesn't matter.
Because someone,
finally selected a complimentary uniform.
Not one that accentuates muffin tops, bulges and
misshapes,
curvaceous Beyonce contours,
or slim Taylor Swift type height and weight.
A black dress;
with short sleeves, proper open neck,
and an A-line design,
one that flatters every shape and dimension.
Regardless if she wears a double zero,
or a queen size.

But that's not what really caught my eye.
She had the moves,
rhythm,
spinning the flag,
and posing like vogue
with her head held high,
her hand on her hip,

a flaunting attitude,
a presence;
in sync with the music.
Proving,
when it comes to swagger,
size
doesn't matter.

♪ ♪ *2nd Prize Winner of the 2017 James and
Christian LaRoche Memorial Poetry Contest*

It's Been A Long Time Coming

God had to scare him into taking his rightful place.
It wasn't easy for him to accept his calling,
A praying man
Bishop TP Johnson
It's been a long time coming.

A fighting Georgia boy from the streets of Cedartown;
Shooting craps, clubbing,
Drinking and dancing with Betty Wright,
Who would have thought
He would be in the church preaching & teaching
Trying to get people to do right.

Some call him flamboyant:
A fancy dresser
With coordinating suit, shirt, and shoes,
Maybe a *Derby* and cane to match,
He loves cologne and his scent trails over
into the pews.

Like most of us, he has his sins:
Diet Coke and *Danny's Fried Chicken,*
But God made some amends,
TP's Georgia Peach, children and grandchildren
Are never too far out of his reach.

He has been misunderstood.
Maybe, he has said some things
That were not so good.
A sensitive man,
He's not too big to recant
His erroneous words that sometimes sting.

He has a song in his heart
That he desires to sing,
A preacher and a teacher
Bishop TP Johnson
It's been a long time coming.

Prince, Into The Cosmos

Surfing online, I went blank
on what I was trying to find.
'Cause a black and white picture of Prince
holding a guitar
with a ghost of smoke hovering
over his left side
surfaced up with the caption
Pop superstar Prince dies at 57!
It was labeled **AP** Associated Press,
so this was no jest.

I yelled, "What, Prince died!"
Needing additional proof,
I turned on the tube to CNN
and Brooke Baldwin had a panel of three
discussing Prince and his legacy.

Back in 1984 or 85,
at the Purple Rain Tour,
I watched Prince strumming his guitar like Jimi Hendrix,
dancing and prancing,
doing the splits,
James Browning across the stage,
and changing into countless outfits
of ruffled shirts, tight pants, and four inch high heels,

giving a spectacular performance.

Fast forward to an awards show
not too long ago.
Prince, scaled from his deep register,
rising into a flawless falsetto.
With his black lined eyes clenched closed,
he was totally spaced out into the cosmos,
caressing and pressing his lady guitar,
fingers ripping and zipping the strings.

Singer, songwriter, producer;
this multi-gifted instrumentalist,
will truly be missed.

Female Folk Favor Fellowship

"I'll always love my mama"
streamed on the radio,
and reminded me of Mama's delicious dishes
that to this day, I can't duplicate,
but definitely miss.

"Jojo, are you sleep?"
"What do you *think*?"
My trickster sister used to lure me to speak,
and I'd end up in conversation with forty winks.

My oldest friend doesn't stroke my ego
with lies and compliments.
She speaks the gospel that I can't forgo,
and makes a whole lot of sense.

We female folk favor fellowship,
come equipped in all shapes and sizes,
with personalities like feisty, poised, witty, and shy,
along with problems and anxieties.

Like Ms. Lula said, God filled the prescription
with gifts of the Word
to sooth our souls,
and prevent annoying conniptions.

Sure, we have some drama queens,
that make you want to scream.
Some of us hold grudges,
and are easily provoked to be mean.

But, we can give a sensitive ear
and listen to the same story
repeatedly, without wanting to fix it or disappear,
even though we may be bored to tears.

I don't want to think of a time
when I'm alone without mama, friend, or sister.
That's why God stirred the pot
and added auntie, granddaughter, niece,
cousin, co-worker, and boss, to the mixture.

A Common End

On my way to the AMC Theater,
the fragrant aroma of chocolate and sweets assaulted
me, making my mouth water for fudge,
as I walked past Kilwins at the Destin Commons.
Nothing like the hypnotizing smell
of baking bread, pepperoni, and garlic,
to introduce the Redbrick Pizza Cafe.

I came upon a man and woman
sitting on a bench in front of it.
He was licking a vanilla ice cream cone,
and she had her head bent, digging a spoon in a cup.
"If you sit down, I can push you,"
he said, making me an offer I would refuse.
I laughed and said,
"That's what my husband always says."

What must I look like, bent over,
pushing my walker and hobbling along,
as if I'm wearing a fin?
"Thanks, but I need the exercise."
We exchanged pleasantries,
talked about movies I've seen,
and I confessed that a lot of people
offer to help me. Especially women,

even if they're accompanied by men.

The woman griped, "People aren't chivalrous
any more." But I let her know
that although, many men are on a mission,
looking straight ahead, minds set on an errand,
chivalry is still alive.
And despite given a bad rap,
young people often offer assistance.

My husband came along after parking the car,
so I told him about the proposal for a lift.
He smiled and agreed he too does this.
We bid them farewell
and headed to the ticket platform.
There we saw a long time acquaintance
and made conversation.

Just as we were set to buy our movie tickets,
the "pusher" guy handed me a gift,
said, "After talking with you,
we're going to see Woodlawn, too.
Here's some tickets. Use the money
you were going to spend,
and give a donation to your church."

We found our seats,

and as usual, I ate $15/16^{th}$ of the large popcorn.
I laughed, I cried, I panicked.
I hoped, I prayed, I was jubilant.
As the credits rolled, my "pusher" friend
came over and thanked me
for sharing the film.

That's when I knew
that it wasn't about me.
Everything was orchestrated:
my limp,
my ability to talk with strangers,
and being distracted by a friend.
All for a common end;
to share the goodness of God.

It was all for Him.

Author Bio

Jocelyn G. Donahoo is a medically retired nurse, now author/spoken word artist. She has poetry and short stories published in the Northwest Florida State College Blackwater Review, recipient of the James and Christian LaRoche Memorial Poetry Contests: 2016 1st prize for *We Called Him Mr. Foster*, and 2017 2nd prize for *Not Your Average Color Guard*, and the 2016 Editor's Prize for Poetry. Author of the novella, *The Cookie Cutter House*, she's currently working on the sequel.

She's happily married to her husband Carl a.k.a "Honey" and lives on Florida's panhandle. They are the proud parents of 4 sons, 3 daughter-in-laws, 7 grandsons, 4 granddaughters, and a foster grandson and granddaughter. She loves Jesus Christ, the arts, yoga, and spends a great deal of time reading and honing her craft.

Made in the USA
Coppell, TX
22 April 2024

31577780R00056